Bajo las olas/Under the Sea

Ballenas/Whales

por/by Carol K. Lindeen

Traducción/Translation: Dr. Martín Luis Guzmán Ferrer
Editor Consultor/Consulting Editor: Dra. Gail Saunders-Smith

Consultor/Consultant: Jody Rake, Member
Southwest Marine/Aquatic Educator's Association

Capstone press®

Mankato, Minnesota

Pebble Plus is published by Capstone Press,
151 Good Counsel Drive, P.O. Box 669, Mankato, Minnesota 56002.
www.capstonepress.com

1 2 3 4 5 6 13 12 11 10 09 08

Library of Congress Cataloging-in-Publication Data
Lindeen, Carol, 1976–
    [Whales. Spanish & English]
    Ballenas / por Carol K. Lindeen = Whales / by Carol K. Lindeen.
    p. cm. — (Bajo las olas = Under the sea)
    Includes index.
    ISBN-13: 978-1-4296-2285-1 (hardcover)
    ISBN-10: 1-4296-2285-7 (hardcover)
    1. Whales — Juvenile literature. I. Title. II. Title: Whales. III. Series.
QL737.C4L5618 2009
599.5 — dc22
                      2008001454

Summary: Simple text and photographs present the lives of whales — in both English and Spanish.

Editorial Credits
Martha E. H. Rustad, editor; Katy Kudela, bilingual editor; Eida del Risco, Spanish copy editor; Juliette Peters,
    designer; Kelly Garvin, photo researcher

Photo Credits
Bruce Coleman Inc./Masa Ushioda–V&W, 18–19
Corbis/Marty Snyderman, 1
Minden Pictures/Flip Nicklin, 6–7, 8–9, 16–17; Mike Parry, cover
PhotoDisc Inc., back cover
Seapics.com/Doug Perrine, 20–21; Kike Calvo/V&W, 12–13; Phillip Colla, 10–11; Masa Ushioda, 4–5, 14–15

Note to Parents and Teachers

The Bajo las olas/Under the Sea set supports national science standards related to the
diversity and unity of life. This book describes and illustrates whales in both English and
Spanish. The images support early readers in understanding the text. The repetition of
words and phrases helps early readers learn new words. This book also introduces early
readers to subject-specific vocabulary words, which are defined in the Glossary section.
Early readers may need assistance to read some words and to use the Table of Contents,
Glossary, Internet Sites, and Index sections of the book.

Table of Contents

Tabla de contenidos

Whales

What are whales?

Whales are mammals.

Las ballenas

¿Qué son las ballenas?

Las ballenas son mamíferos.

Whales breathe air.
They have blowholes
on top of their heads.

Las ballenas respiran aire.
En la parte de arriba de
la cabeza tienen espiráculos.

7

Smooth skin covers whales.
Blubber under their skin
keeps whales warm.

Las ballenas están cubiertas
de una piel lisa. Bajo la piel
tienen una grasa que
las mantiene calentitas.

Small whales are about
as long as a jump rope.
Big whales can be the
size of a big airplane.

Las ballenas pequeñas son tan
largas como una cuerda de saltar.
Las ballenas grandes pueden ser
del tamaño de un avión.

Swimming

Whales move their strong tails
up and down to swim.

Nadar

Las ballenas mueven sus
fuertes colas de arriba
hacia abajo para nadar.

Most whales have fins
on their backs. Fins help
whales balance. Flippers
help whales steer.

La mayoría de las ballenas tiene
aletas en el lomo. Las aletas
les sirven a las ballenas para
mantener el equilibrio. Las aletas
también les sirven para navegar.

Some whales swim to
warmer water in the fall.
They mate and have young.

Algunas ballenas nadan a
los mares templados en
el otoño. Allí se aparean
y tienen a sus crías.

Whales breach.
Some whales can
jump out of the water.

Las ballenas dan saltos hacia
arriba. Algunas ballenas saltan
fuera del agua.

Under the Sea

Whales swim

under the sea.

Bajo las olas

Las ballenas nadan

bajo las olas.

Glossary

blowhole — an opening on the top of a whale's head; whales breathe air through blowholes.

blubber — a layer of fat under a whale's skin; blubber helps whales stay warm.

breach — to jump out of the water

fin — a thin body part on a swimming animal; most whales have fins on their backs.

flipper — a flat limb with bones on the bodies of some sea animals; whales have two flippers; flippers help whales swim.

mammal — a warm-blooded animal with a backbone that breathes air with lungs; mammals have some hair or fur; female mammals feed milk to their young.

mate — to join together to produce young

steer — to move in a certain direction

Glosario

la aleta — brazo plano con huesos en el cuerpo de algunos animales marinos; las ballenas tienen dos aletas; las aletas ayudan a las ballenas a nadar.

aparearse — juntarse para tener crías

el espiráculo — apertura en la cabeza de las ballenas; las ballenas respiran por estas aperturas.

el mamífero — animal de sangre caliente con columna que respira aire con sus pulmones; los mamíferos tienen piel o pelo; las hembras de los mamíferos alimentan a sus crías con leche.

navegar — moverse en el agua en cierta dirección

templado — tibio; que no está ni frío ni caliente.

Internet Sites

FactHound offers a safe, fun way to find Internet sites related to this book. All of the sites on FactHound have been researched by our staff.

Here's how:

1. Visit *www.facthound.com*

2. Choose your grade level.

3. Type in this book ID **1429622857** for age-appropriate sites. You may also browse subjects by clicking on letters, or by clicking on pictures and words.

4. Click on the **Fetch It** button.

FactHound will fetch the best sites for you!

Index

Sitios de Internet

FactHound te brinda una manera divertida y segura de encontrar sitios de Internet relacionados con este libro. Hemos investigado todos los sitios de FactHound. Es posible que algunos sitios no estén en español.

Se hace así:

1. Visita *www.facthound.com*

2. Elige tu grado escolar.

3. Introduce este código especial **1429622857** para ver sitios apropiados a tu edad, o usa una palabra relacionada con este libro para hacer una búsqueda general.

4. Haz un clic en el botón **Fetch It**.

¡FactHound buscará los mejores sitios para ti!

Índice